Montana

By Lisa Trumbauer

Consultant
Jeanne Clidas, Ph.D.
National Reading Consultant
and
Professor of Reading, SUNY Brockport

Children's Press®
A Division of Scholastic Inc.
New York   Toronto   London   Auckland   Sydney
Mexico City   New Delhi   Hong Kong
Danbury, Connecticut

Designer: Herman Adler Design
Photo Researcher: Caroline Anderson
The photo on the cover shows Glacier National Park, Montana.

Library of Congress Cataloging-in-Publication Data

Trumbauer, Lisa, 1963-
  Montana / by Lisa Trumbauer.
    p. cm. – (Rookie read-about geography)
  Summary: A simple introduction to Montana, focusing on its regions and geographical features.
  Includes index.
  ISBN 0-516-22737-8 (lib. bdg.)   0-516-23606-7 (pbk.)
  1. Montana–Juvenile literature. 2. Montana–Geography–Juvenile literature. [1. Montana.] I. Title. II. Series.
  F731.3.T69 2003
  978.6–dc21
                                        2003000369

Do you know why Montana
is called Big Sky Country?

The sky in Montana
looks huge!

Montana is the fourth
largest state. Canada is
north of Montana. Idaho,
Wyoming, North Dakota,
and South Dakota are
around Montana.

CANADA

WASHINGTON

MONTANA

NORTH DAKOTA

MINNESOTA

NEW HAMPSHIRE

VERMONT

MAINE

OREGON

IDAHO

WYOMING

SOUTH DAKOTA

WISCONSIN

MICHIGAN

NEW YORK

MASSACHUSETTS

RHODE ISLAND

CONNECTICUT

NEVADA

UTAH

NEBRASKA

IOWA

ILLINOIS

INDIANA

OHIO

PENNSYLVANIA

NEW JERSEY

DELAWARE

WEST VIRGINIA

MARYLAND

CALIFORNIA

COLORADO

KANSAS

MISSOURI

KENTUCKY

VIRGINIA

Washington, D.C.

ARIZONA

NEW MEXICO

OKLAHOMA

ARKANSAS

TENNESSEE

NORTH CAROLINA

SOUTH CAROLINA

TEXAS

MISSISSIPPI

ALABAMA

GEORGIA

LOUISIANA

FLORIDA

ALASKA

CANADA

MEXICO

HAWAII

North

West

East

South

Montana is a land of mountains and plains.

The Great Plains cover much of eastern Montana. In the spring, wild flowers grow on the grassy plains.

The word *montaña* means "mountain" in Spanish.

The Rocky Mountains cross western Montana.

Some people come to
Montana to dig for dinosaur
(DYE-nuh-sor) bones.

Even T-Rex skeletons
have been found in
Montana. Another name
for Tyrannosaurus Rex
(tuh-RAN-uh-sor-uhs reks)
is T-Rex. Can you say that?

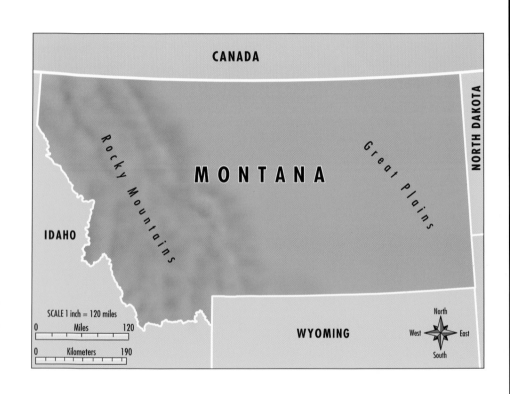

People fishing in the Sun River

Montana has many
Two of these rivers
Missouri River an
Yellowstone Rive

People visiting
to fish in the r

S
N
(I

Se
hav
Mo
for
(ti-P
is T-

A model of a T-Rex

Today, you would not
see dinosaurs in Montana.
You might see a grizzly
bear. It is the state animal.

Grizzly bear

Western meadowlark

The western meadowlark
(MED-oh-lark) is the
state bird.

The capital of Montana
is Helena.

The largest city is Billings.
Nearly 90,000 people live
in Billings.

Billings

The cities and towns in Montana are not very close together. People drive a long way to shop or visit friends.

Railroads also help to bring people and things from place to place.

Miners dig for coal, gas, and other things.

A piece of coal

Mining for coal

Montana mines the
most talc. Talc is used
to make powder.

Farms and ranches in Montana are big. They are bigger than anywhere else in the United States.

About one out of ten people in Montana are farmers or ranchers.

Most people work in grocery stores, department stores, or restaurants.

Many people in Montana
also work in state parks.
A state park is run by
the government.

Montana has more than
forty state parks.

Maybe someday you can see the mountains and plains of Montana.

You will never forget your visit to Big Sky Country!

Words You Know

Billings

coal

dinosaur

grizzly bear

meadowlark

mining

mountains

ranch

31

Index

About the Author

Lisa Trumbauer has written nearly 200 books for children. She lives with her husband, two cats, and one dog in Hillsborough, New Jersey. She loves to travel and write about the United States.

Photo Credits

Photographs © 2003: Chuck Haney: 17, 22, 30 top left, 31 bottom right; Dembinsky Photo Assoc./Stan Osolinski: 13, 30 bottom left; John Reddy: cover, 3, 10, 19, 25, 26, 28; Photo Researchers, NY: 6, 14, 30 bottom right, 31 bottom left (Stephen J. Krasemann), 15, 31 top left (Rod Planck); The Image Works/Townsend P. Dickinson: 20, 30 top right; Visuals Unlimited/Paul Dix: 21, 31 top right.

Maps by Bob Italiano

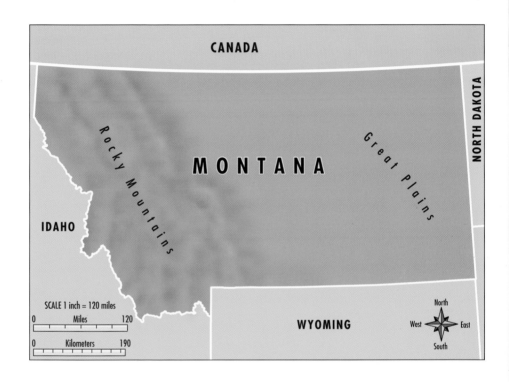

CANADA

CANADA

NORTH DAKOTA

Rocky Mountains

MONTANA

Great Plains

IDAHO

SCALE 1 inch = 120 miles

0   Miles   120

0   Kilometers   190

WYOMING

North
West ✦ East
South

9

People fishing in the Sun River

Montana has many rivers. Two of these rivers are the Missouri River and the Yellowstone River.

People visiting Montana like to fish in the rivers.

Some people come to Montana to dig for dinosaur (DYE-nuh-sor) bones.

Seven T-Rex skeletons have been found in Montana. Another name for Tyrannosaurus Rex (ti-RAN-uh-sor-uhs reks) is T-Rex. Can you say that?